ZeNSpiRAtiONS®

Expressions of Faith

CREATE, COLOR, PATTERN, PLAY!

JOANNE FINK

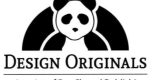

DESIGN ORIGINALS

an Imprint of Fox Chapel Publishing
www.d-originals.com

Zenspirations® Patterning Basics

The illustrations in this book are designed to be a springboard for *your* creativity—that's why there is a credit line for you, as co-creator, at the bottom of each page. Before you start to color, take a moment to review some of my favorite patterns, which you can use to enhance the designs. In addition to embellishing what's already on the page, I encourage you to express what's in your heart by adding your own text and illustrations to the designs. I've given you step-by-step instructions.

Patterns: Step-by-Step Examples

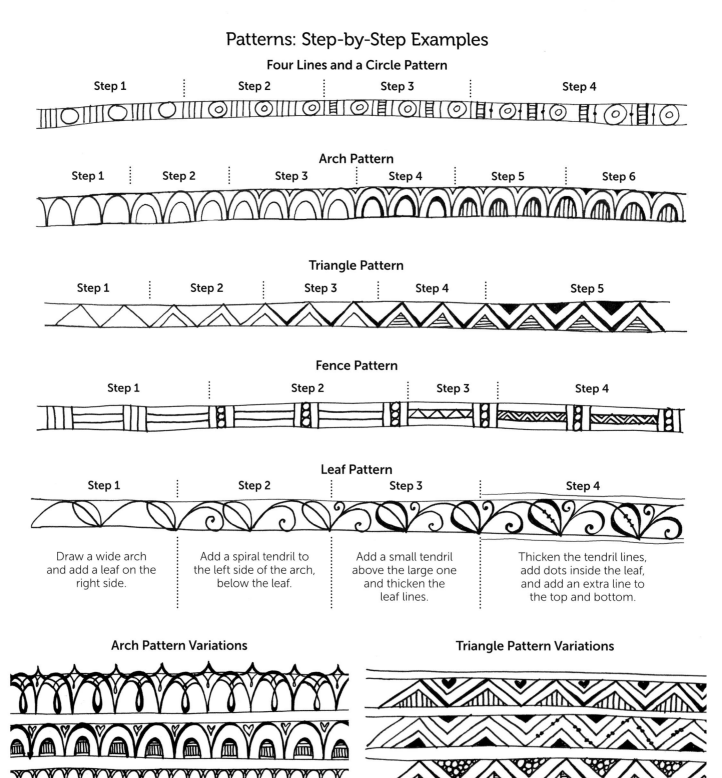

Four Lines and a Circle Pattern
Step 1   Step 2   Step 3   Step 4

Arch Pattern
Step 1   Step 2   Step 3   Step 4   Step 5   Step 6

Triangle Pattern
Step 1   Step 2   Step 3   Step 4   Step 5

Fence Pattern
Step 1   Step 2   Step 3   Step 4

Leaf Pattern
Step 1   Step 2   Step 3   Step 4

Draw a wide arch and add a leaf on the right side.

Add a spiral tendril to the left side of the arch, below the leaf.

Add a small tendril above the large one and thicken the leaf lines.

Thicken the tendril lines, add dots inside the leaf, and add an extra line to the top and bottom.

Arch Pattern Variations

Triangle Pattern Variations

Zenspirations® Create, Color, Pattern, Play pages are designed to allow your creativity to shine. You can color each page as-is, or make the design your own by adding patterns and embellishing the illustration.

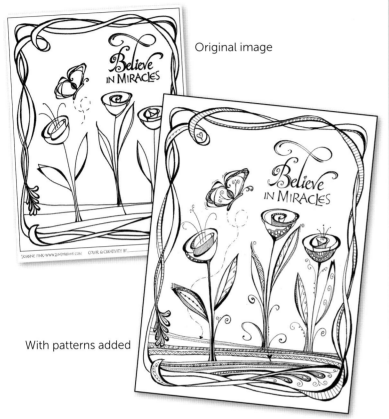

Original image

With patterns added

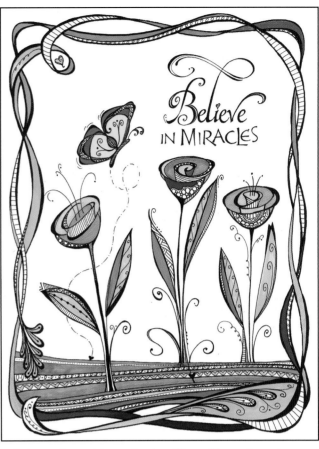

Color and creativity enthusiast Alison Clement used pens to add patterns, then used brush markers to add color to the design.

Adding Patterns: Step-by-Step Example

Here are a few simple techniques for enhancing an existing illustration with patterns. You can add as little or as much as you want—be creative!

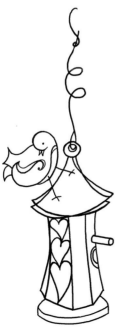

Original image

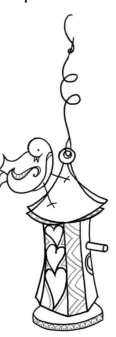

Step 1: Add patterns in the open spaces.

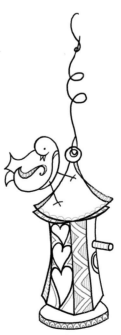

Step 2: Add extra details within the patterns.

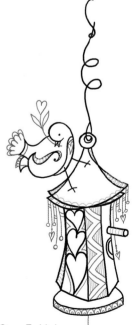

Step 3: Make the design your own by adding on to the existing illustration.

Zenspirations® Drawing Basics

You can use a similar step-by-step method to create additional elements to add to one of the pages in this book, or combine several simple drawings to create your own design.

Try drawing and patterning the cloud, snail, and flower icons below. Notice how they are incorporated into the scene on the next page. Practice creating a similar scene using your favorite icons.

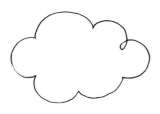

Step 1: Draw the shape.

Step 2: Add lines to create spaces around the perimeter.

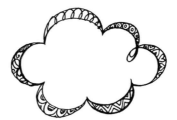

Step 3: Add patterns inside the perimeter spaces to create interest.

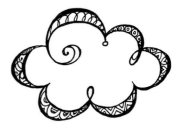

Step 4: Finish by adding weight to the exterior lines. If desired, enhance by adding your own special touches, such as the spiral, dot, and loops in the cloud and the face and antennae in the snail.

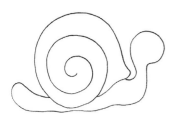
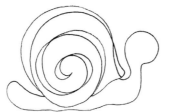
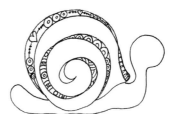
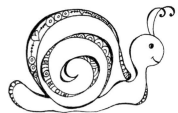

How to Draw a Funky Flower

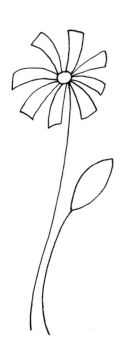
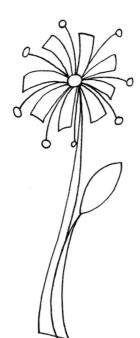
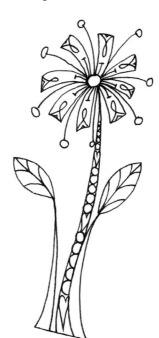
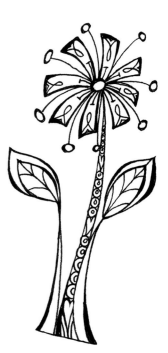

Step 1: Start with a simple drawing.

Step 2: Add a line with a circle at the end between each petal. Add a second line to fill out the stem and leaf.

Step 3: Add small, simple patterns to the petals, leaves, and stem.

Step 4: Finish by thickening some of the lines.

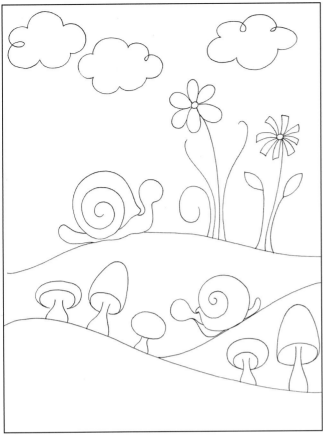

Step 1: Draw the scene.

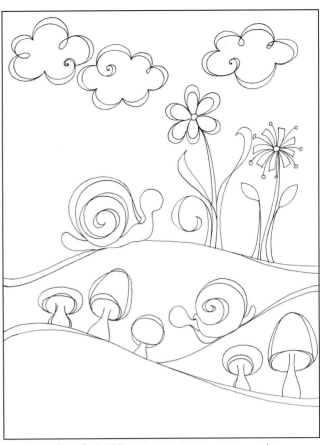

Step 2: Add lines to create spaces around the perimeter of each icon.

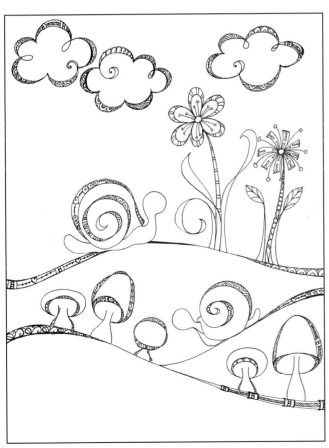

Step 3: Add patterns inside the perimeter spaces to create interest.

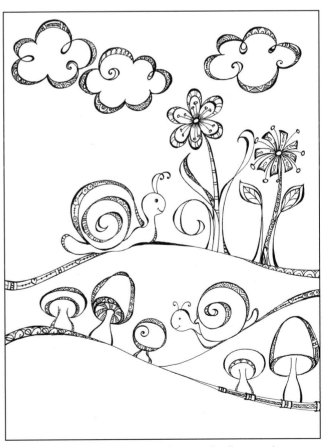

Step 4: Add weight to the exterior lines and finish by adding your own special touches.

Making the Design Your Own

The same design can be interpreted many different ways. You can adapt the designs in this book as little or as much as you want—be creative! Here are some examples for inspiration.

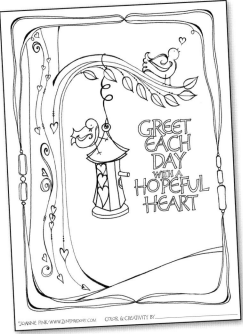

Original image

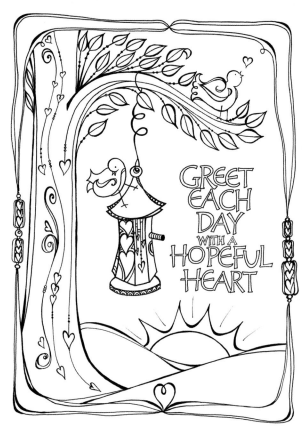

Variation 1: Patterning added to birdhouse and beads; leaves added to tree; hill and sun added to landscape; heart added to bottom border.

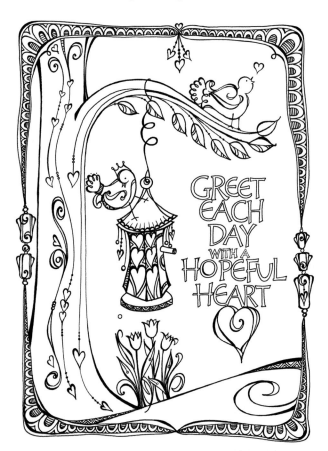

Variation 2: Patterning and dangles added to birdhouse and border; patterning added to leaves; feathers added to birds; flowers added below birdhouse; swirl added to hill; heart added below lettering.

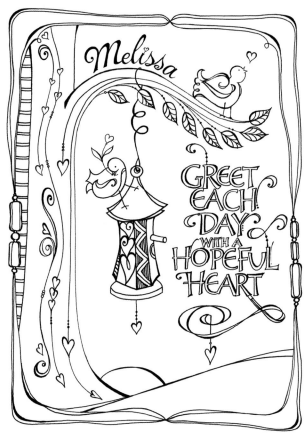

Variation 3: Enhanced lettering with dangles and flourish; name added above branch; flower added in bird's mouth; patterning added to leaves; sun added to landscape; patterning added to left side of tree trunk.

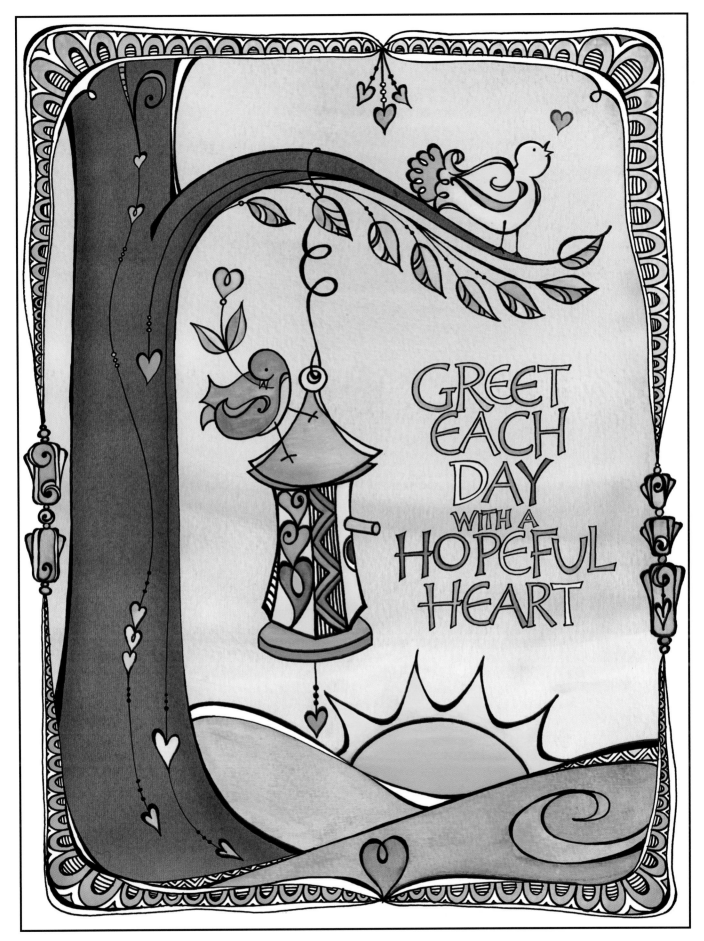

GREET EACH DAY WITH A HOPEFUL HEART

COLOR & CREATIVITY BY _____

Special thanks to color and creativity enthusiast Samantha Trattner for her lovely watercolor version of this design.

Zenspirations® Coloring Basics

The icons on these pages have been colored and patterned using different coloring mediums, each producing different effects. I recommend experimenting with different mediums on scrap paper to help find the ones you prefer before applying them to your designs.

Don't feel like you must color every part of a design. I often leave a few areas of white in my images, especially in the patterns.

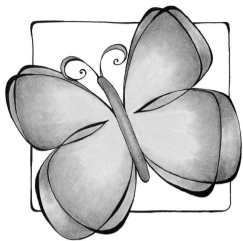

Colored with colored pencils. Blended with artist odorless mineral spirits and blending stump.

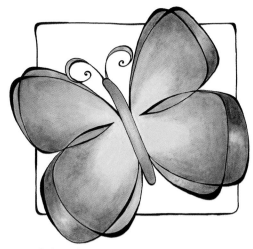

Colored with water-soluble pencils. Blended with blender brush pen.

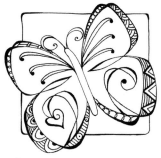

Patterned with black pen.

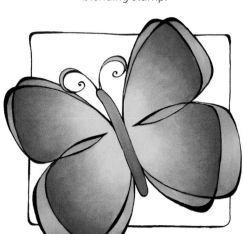

Colored with alcohol markers.
Color by Sandy Allnock.

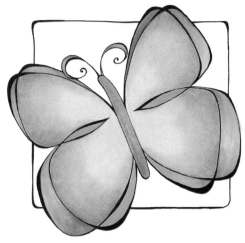

Colored with colored pencils and brush pens.

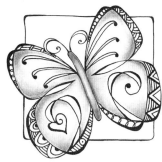

Patterned with black pen. Shaded with graphite pencil.

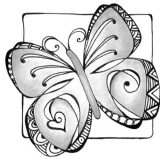

Patterned with black pen. Colored with colored pencils.

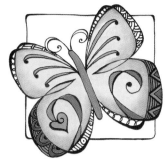

Patterned with black pen. Colored with colored pencils, gel pens, and brush pens.

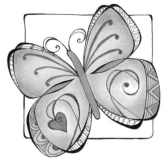

Patterned with colored pens. Colored with colored pencils, brush pens, and colored pens.

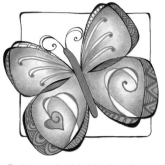

Patterned with black gel pen. Colored with colored pencils and brush pens.

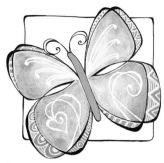

Patterned with white gel pen. Colored with water-soluble pencils and brush pens.

Special thanks to Jo-Ellen Mathews for the patterned and colored butterfly samples.

When I color my designs, I love to contrast areas of matte color with areas that shimmer and shine, and I often add touches of metallic and glitter. I gravitate toward a bright palette, but encourage you to work with whatever colors sing to your soul.

Be sure to check out the finished samples on the next few pages to see how different color and creativity enthusiasts from around the globe interpret the same design.

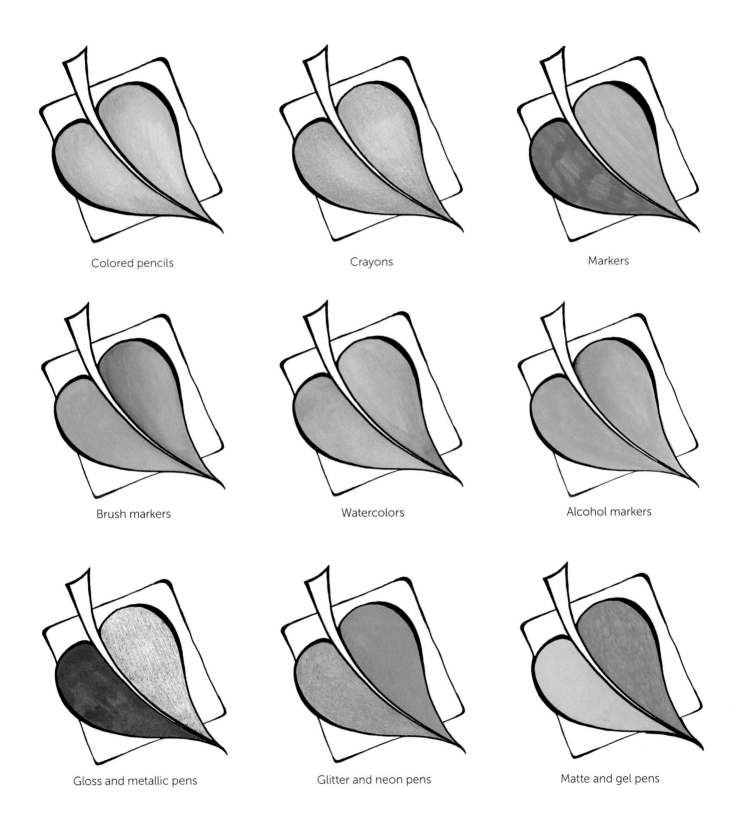

Colored pencils

Crayons

Markers

Brush markers

Watercolors

Alcohol markers

Gloss and metallic pens

Glitter and neon pens

Matte and gel pens

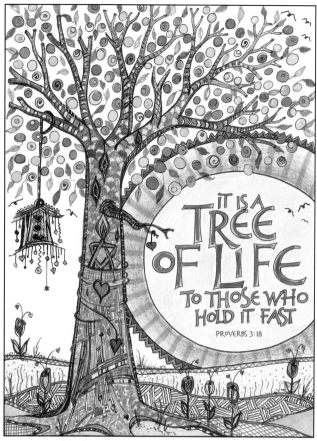

Markers, gel pens, colored pencils.
Color & creativity by Gail Beck.

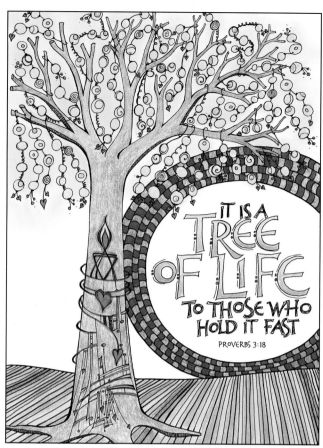

Pastels, colored pencils, markers, pens.
Color & creativity by Karen Stellema.

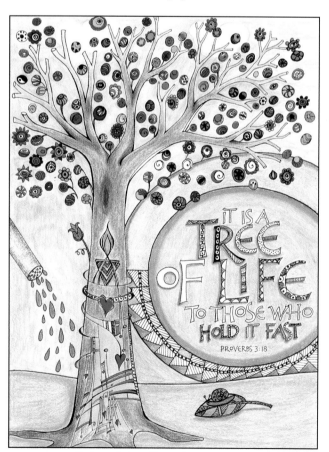

Colored pencils, gel pens, pens.
Color & creativity by Puneet Sekhon.

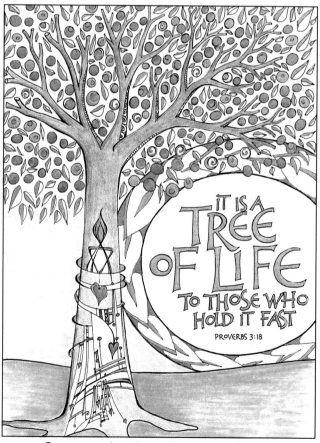

Crayons, colored pencils, pens, gel pens.
Color & creativity by Lora Trapp.

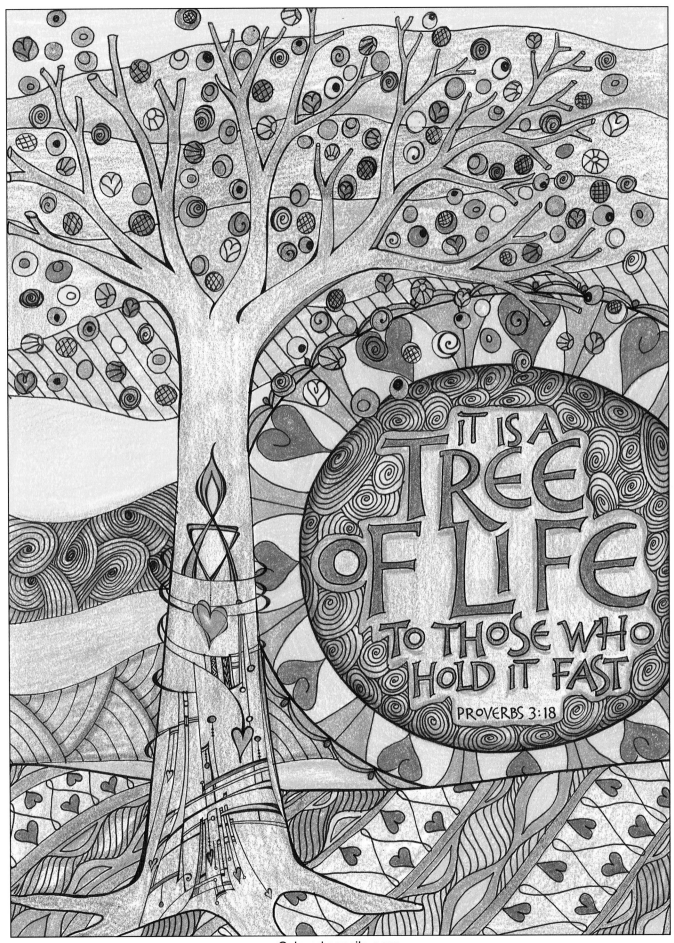

IT IS A TREE OF LIFE TO THOSE WHO HOLD IT FAST

PROVERBS 3:18

Colored pencils, pens.
Color & creativity by Terri Brown.

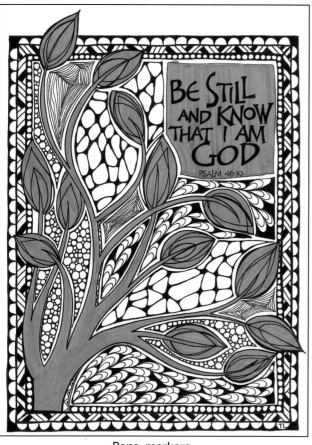

Pens, markers.
Color & creativity by Tracey Lyon.

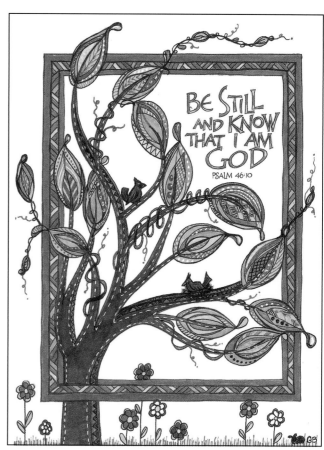

Markers, gel pens.
Color & creativity by Gail Beck.

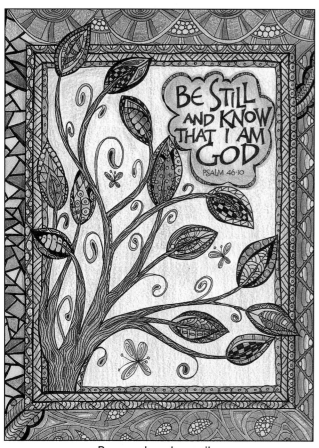

Pens, colored pencils.
Color & creativity by Terri Brown.

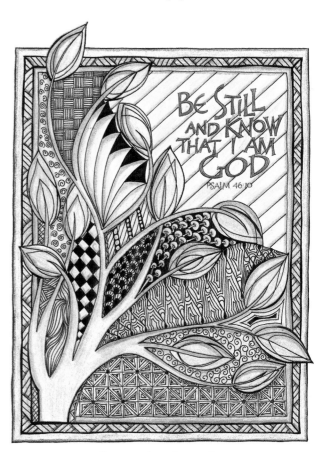

Pens, colored pencils.
Color & creativity by Ardis Ferdig.

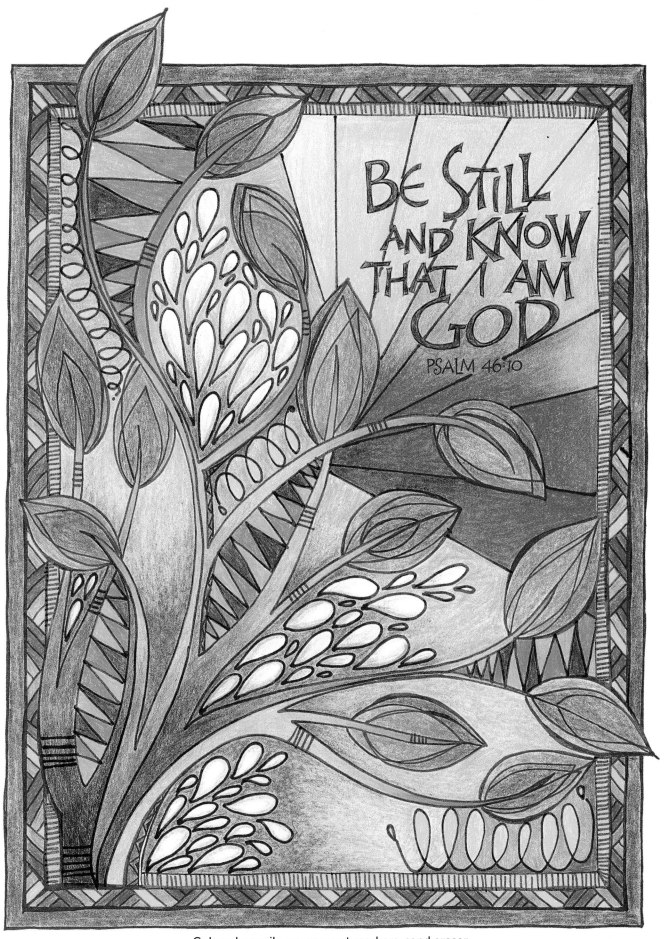

Colored pencils, permanent markers, sand eraser.

Color & creativity by Jennifer Priest.

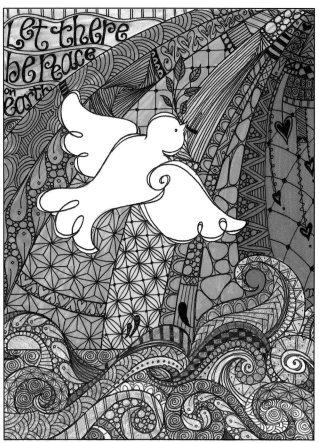

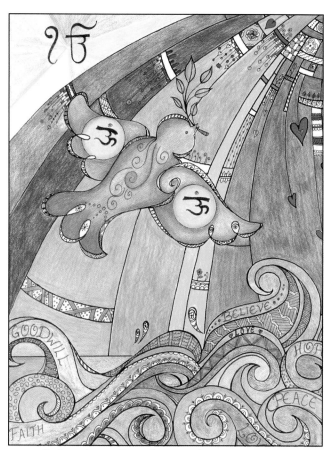

Dual-tip markers, brush markers, pens.
Color & creativity by Tracey Lyon.

Colored pencils, gel pens, glaze pens, pens.
Color & creativity by Puneet Sekhon.

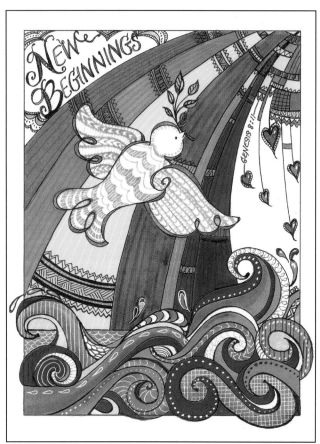

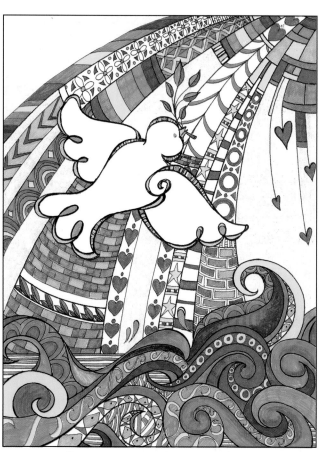

Markers, gel pens.
Color & creativity by Gail Beck.

Crayons, pens, gel pens, markers.
Color & creativity by Lora Trapp.

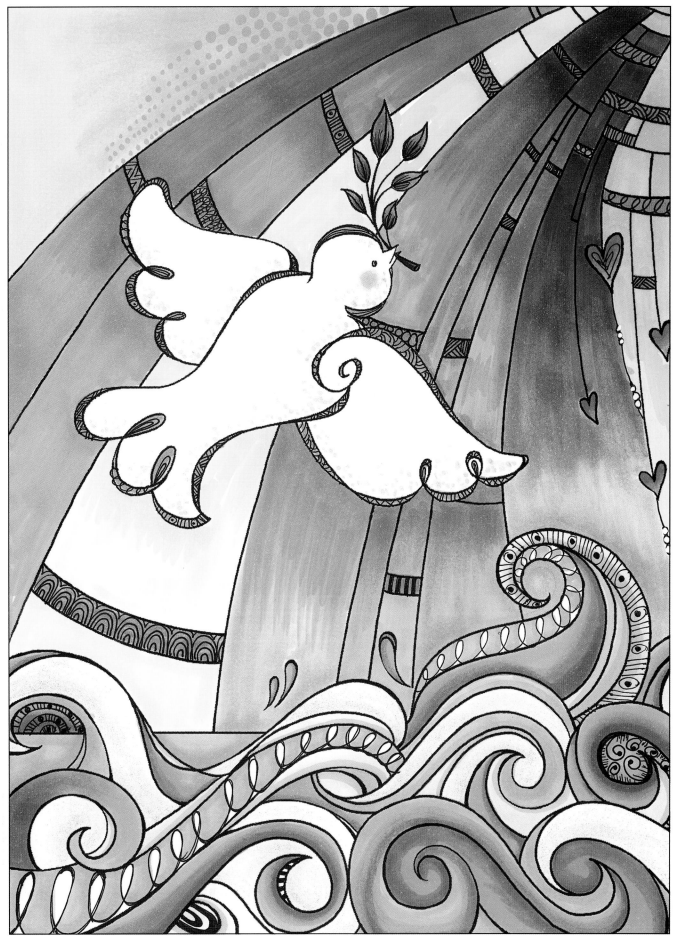

Markers.
Color & creativity by Carisa Zglobicki.

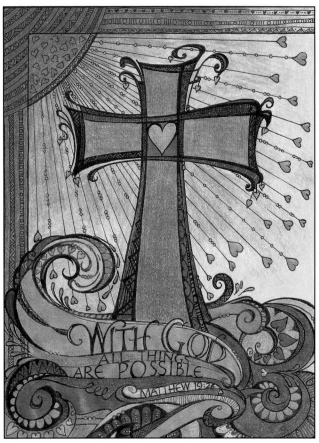

Colored pencils, metallic pens, pens.
Color & creativity by Kathryn Leonard.

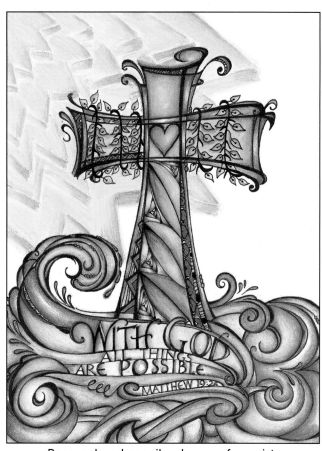

Pens, colored pencils, glue pen for resist.
Color & creativity by Marizaan van Beek.

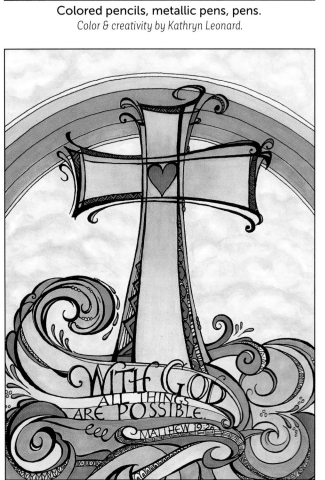

Markers.
Color & creativity by Mary Taylor.

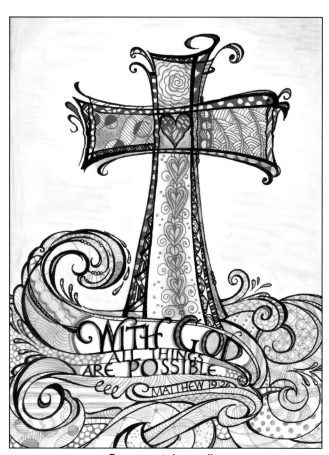

Pens, pastel pencils.
Color & creativity by Rita Barakat.

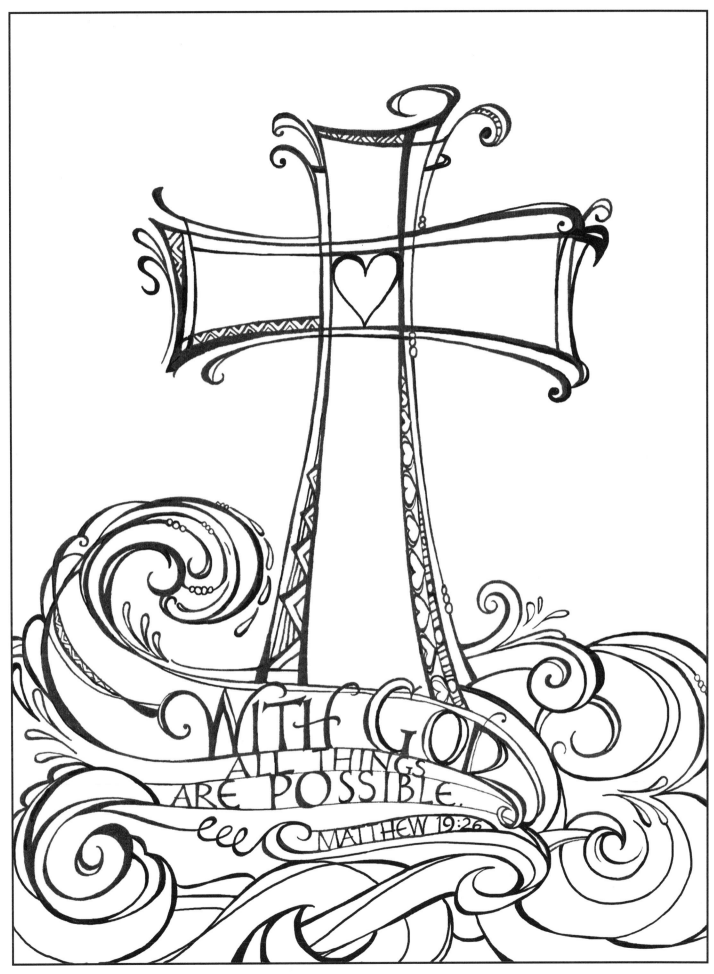

WITH GOD ALL THINGS ARE POSSIBLE. MATTHEW 19:26

COLOR & CREATIVITY BY_____

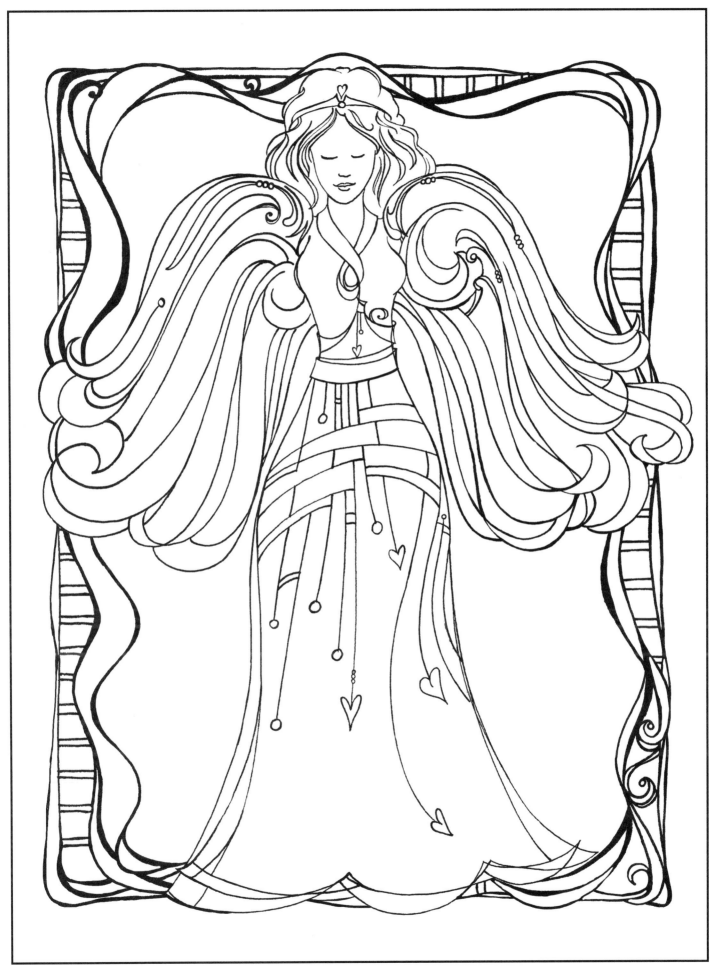

COLOR & CREATIVITY BY_____

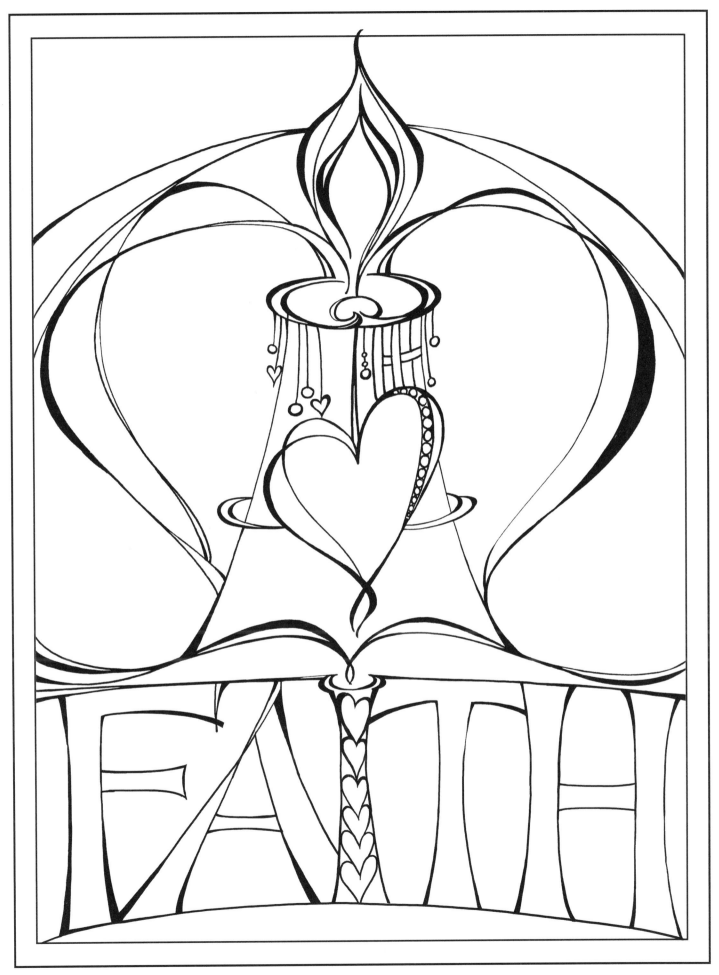

COLOR & CREATIVITY BY_____

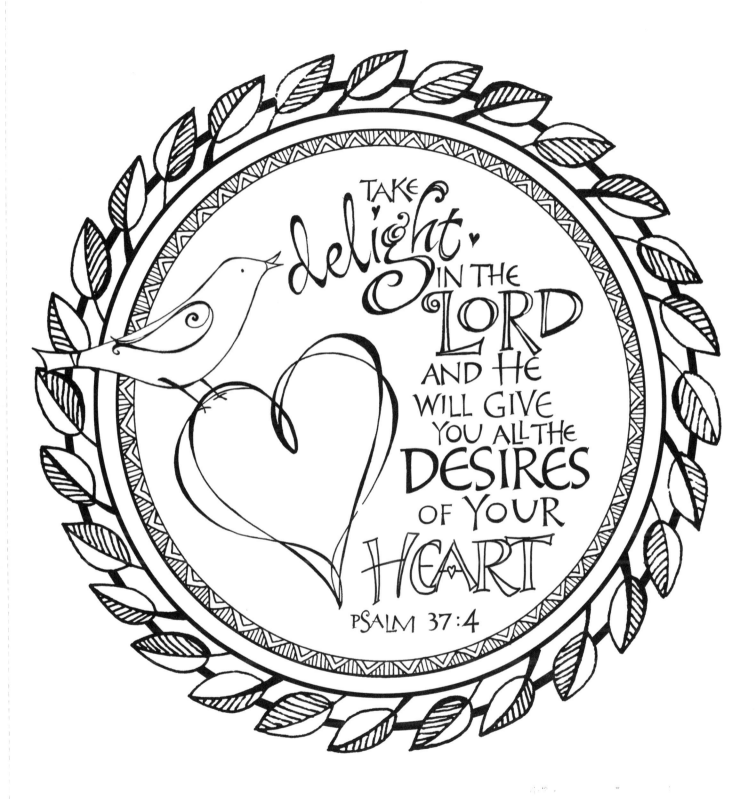

TAKE delight IN THE LORD AND HE WILL GIVE YOU ALL THE DESIRES OF YOUR HEART

PSALM 37:4

COLOR & CREATIVITY BY_____

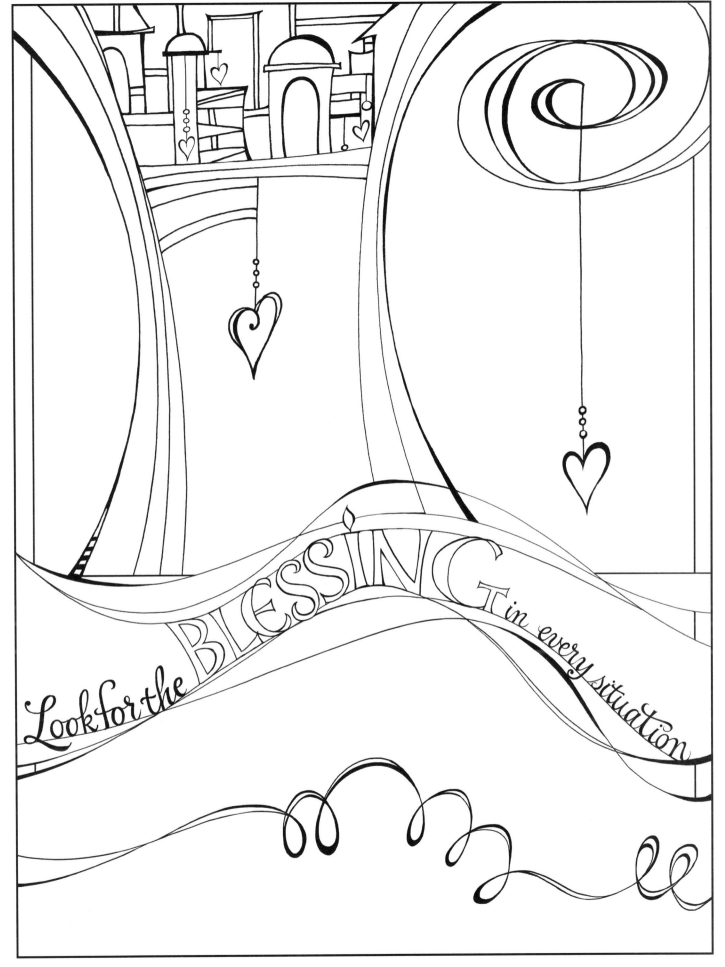

Look for the BLESSING in every situation

COLOR & CREATIVITY BY _____

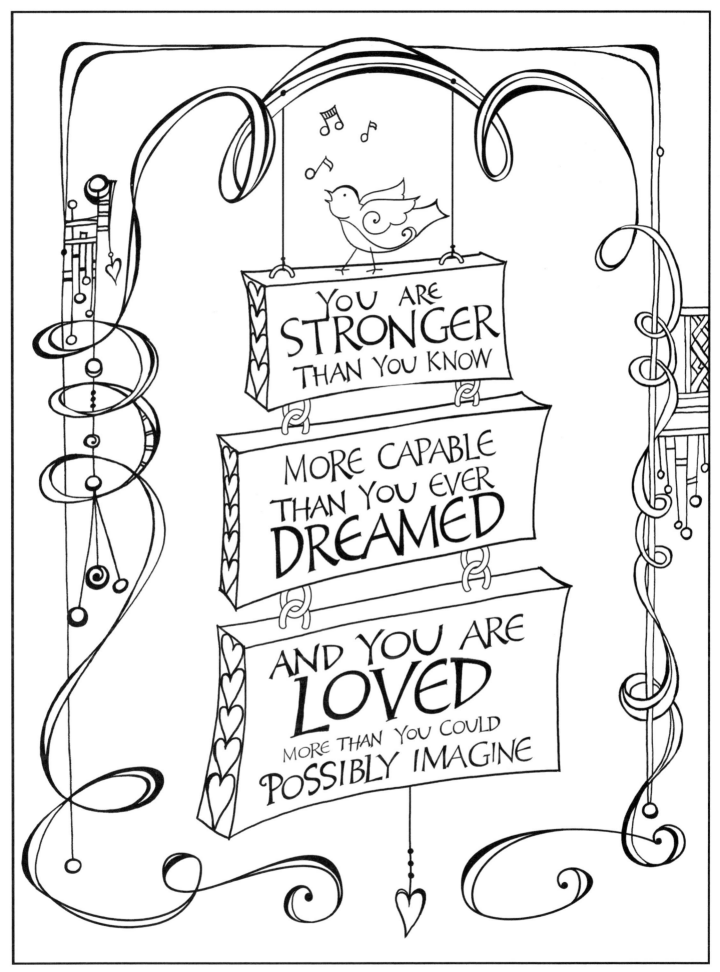

COLOR & CREATIVITY BY_____

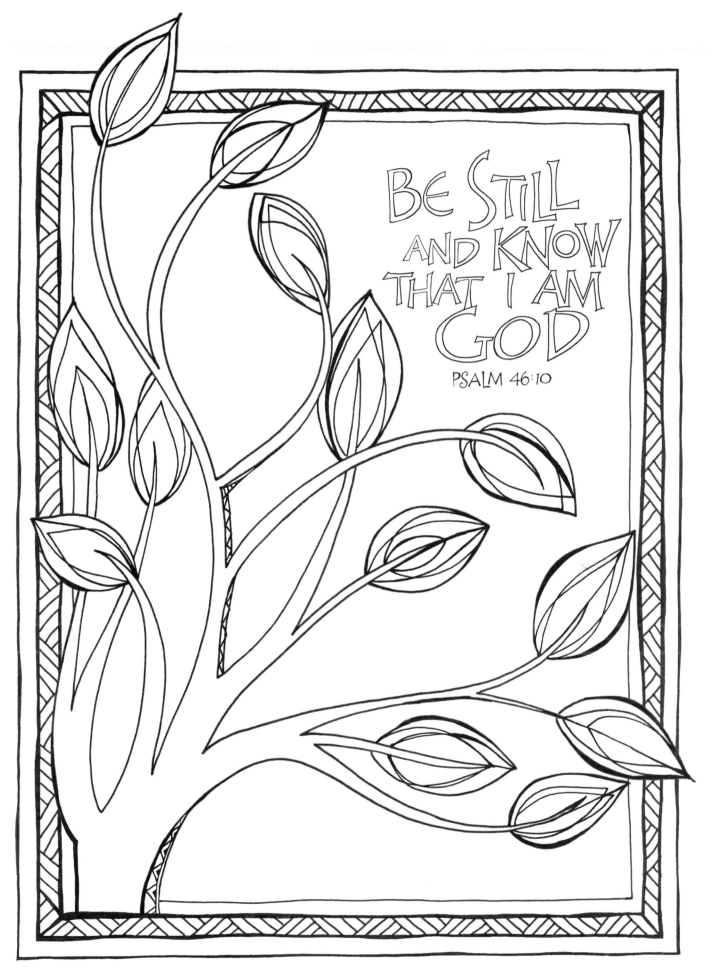

BE STILL
AND KNOW
THAT I AM
GOD

PSALM 46:10

©JOANNE FINK · WWW.ZENSPIRATIONS.COM   COLOR & CREATIVITY BY _____

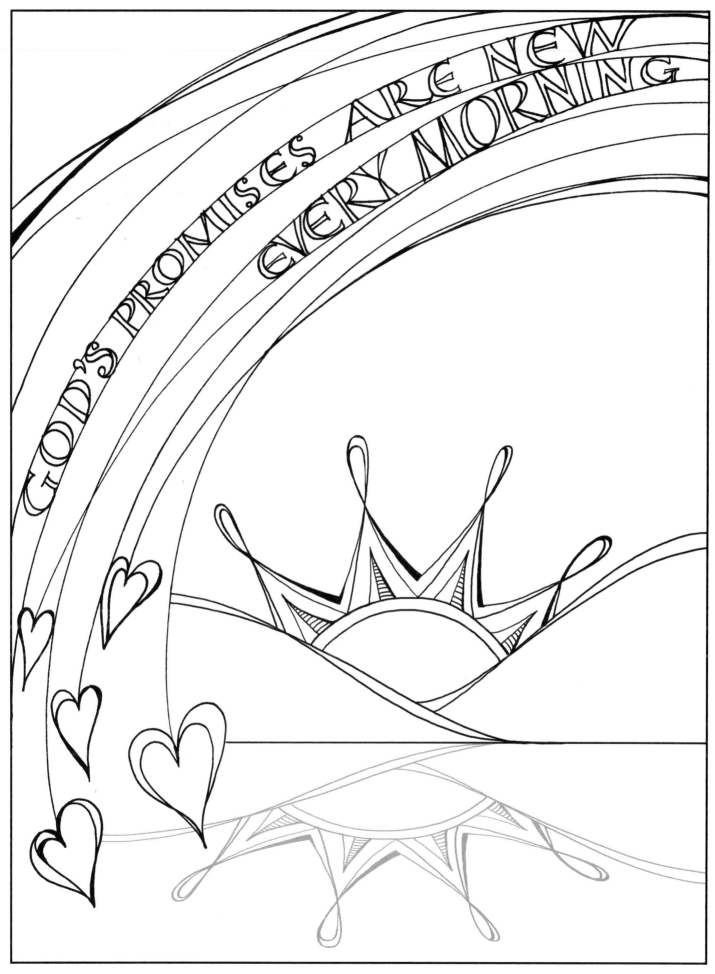

GOD'S PROMISES ARE NEW EVERY MORNING

COLOR & CREATIVITY BY_____

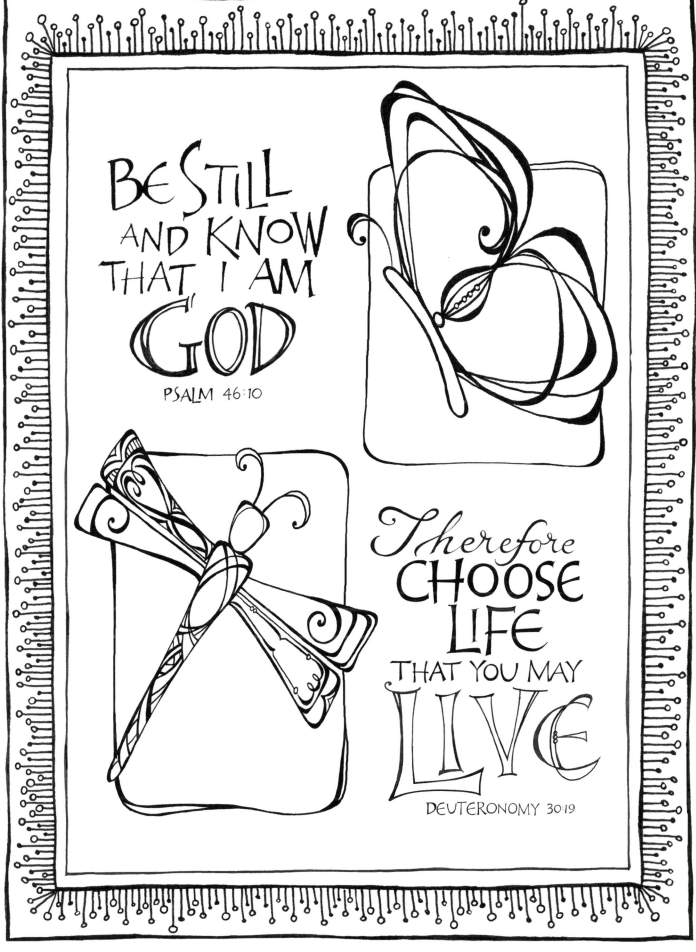

BE STILL AND KNOW THAT I AM GOD

PSALM 46:10

Therefore CHOOSE LIFE THAT YOU MAY LIVE

DEUTERONOMY 30:19

©JOANNE FINK·WWW.ZENSPIRATIONS.COM   COLOR & CREATIVITY BY_____

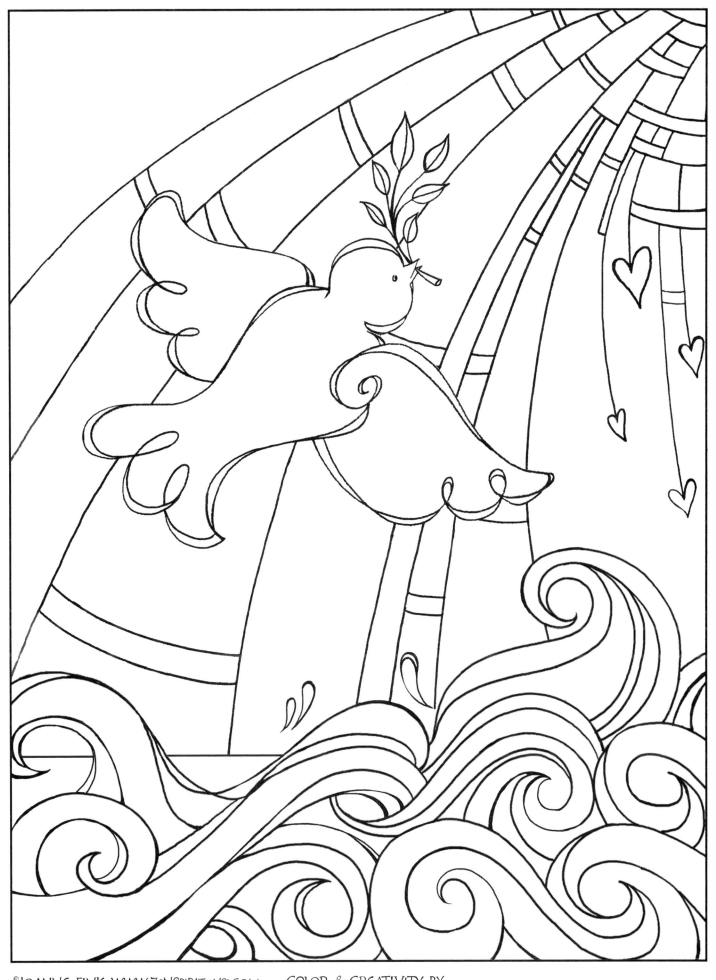

COLOR & CREATIVITY BY_____

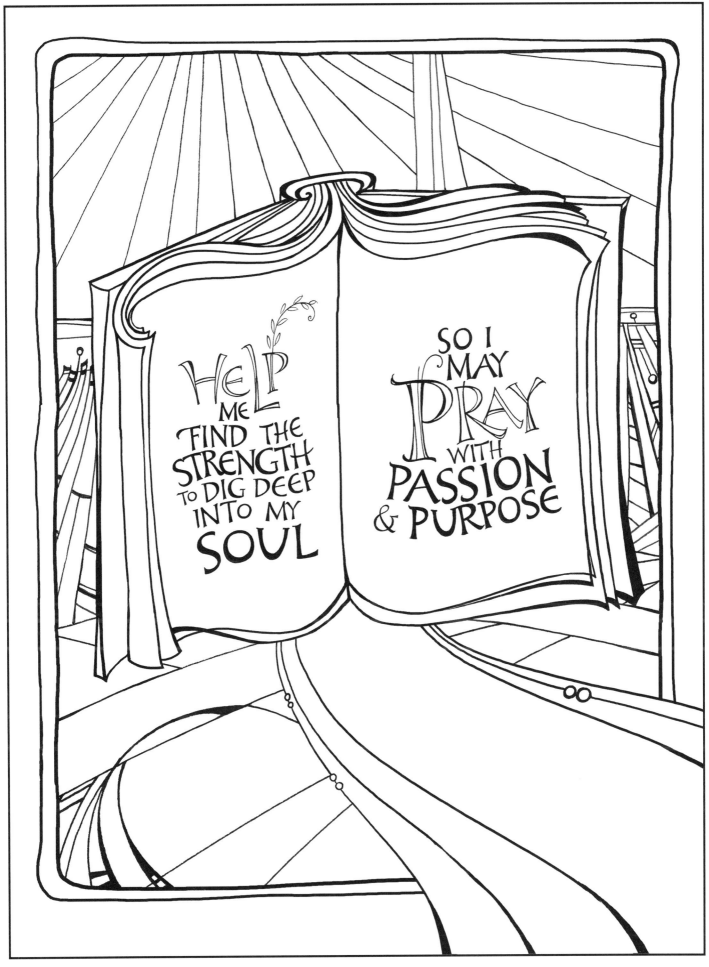

HELP ME FIND THE STRENGTH TO DIG DEEP INTO MY SOUL

SO I MAY PRAY WITH PASSION & PURPOSE

COLOR & CREATIVITY BY_____

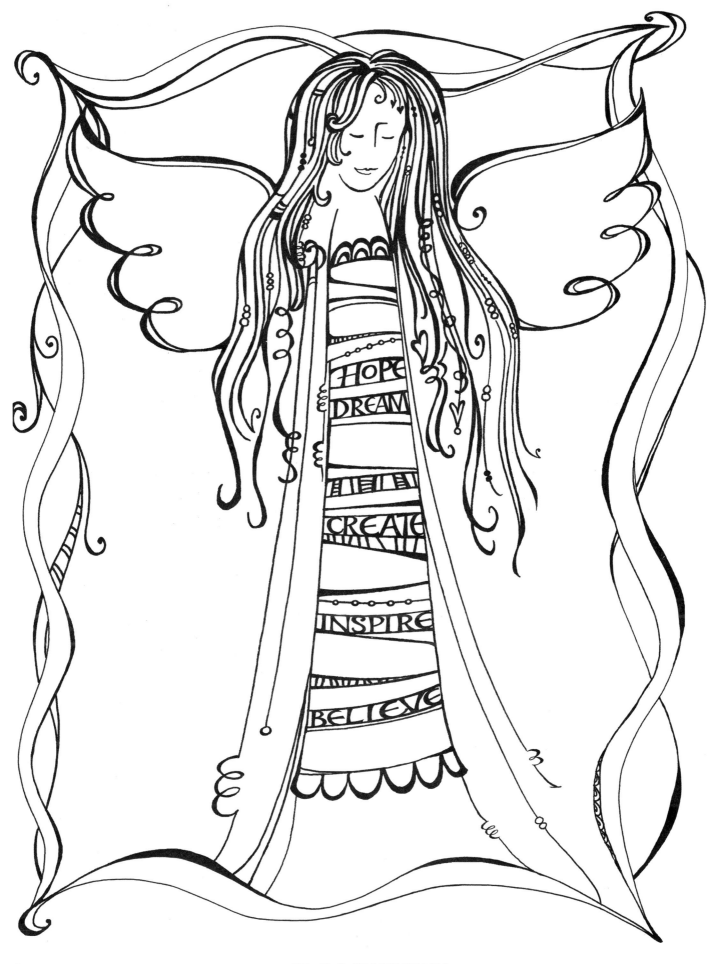

HOPE
DREAM
CREATE
INSPIRE
BELIEVE

©JOANNE FINK·WWW.ZENSPIRATIONS.COM   COLOR & CREATIVITY BY

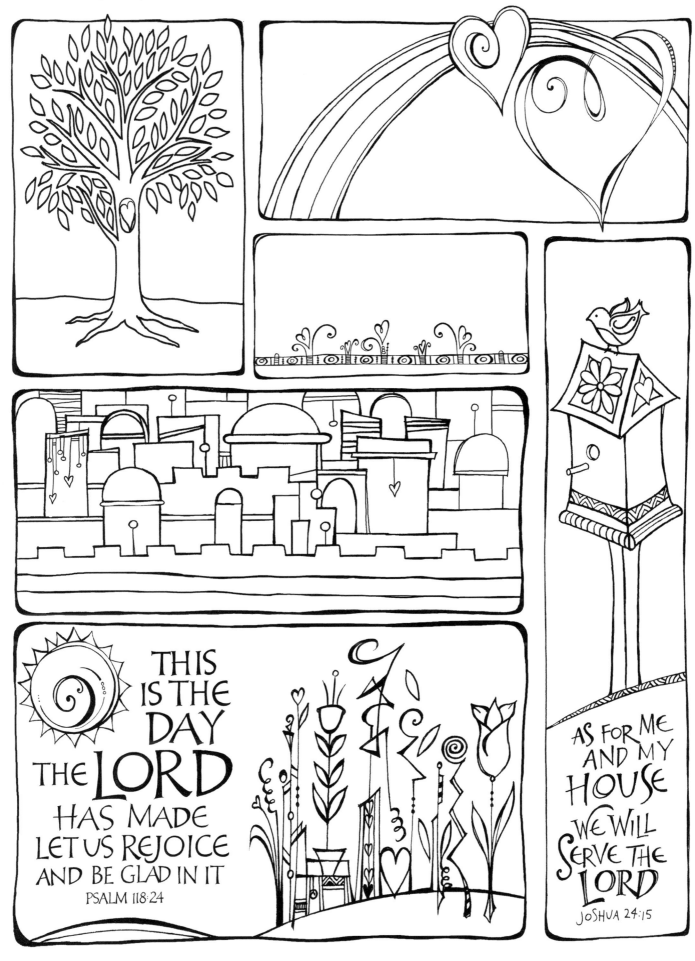

THIS IS THE DAY THE LORD HAS MADE LET US REJOICE AND BE GLAD IN IT
PSALM 118:24

AS FOR ME AND MY HOUSE WE WILL SERVE THE LORD
JOSHUA 24:15

COLOR & CREATIVITY BY_____

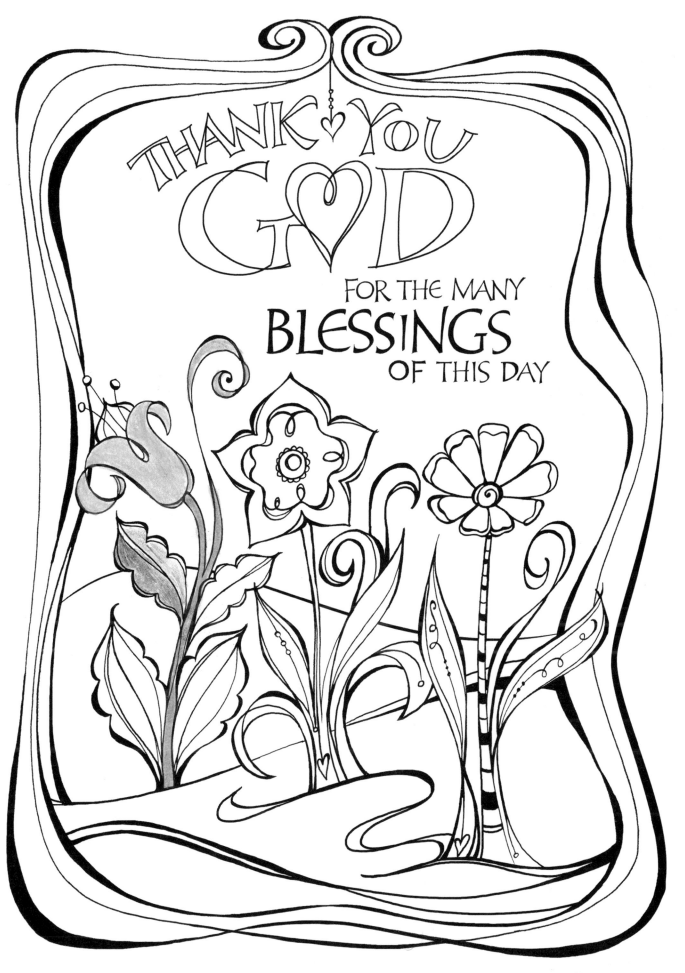

THANK YOU GOD FOR THE MANY BLESSINGS OF THIS DAY

©JOANNE FINK · WWW.ZENSPIRATIONS.COM   COLOR & CREATIVITY BY_____

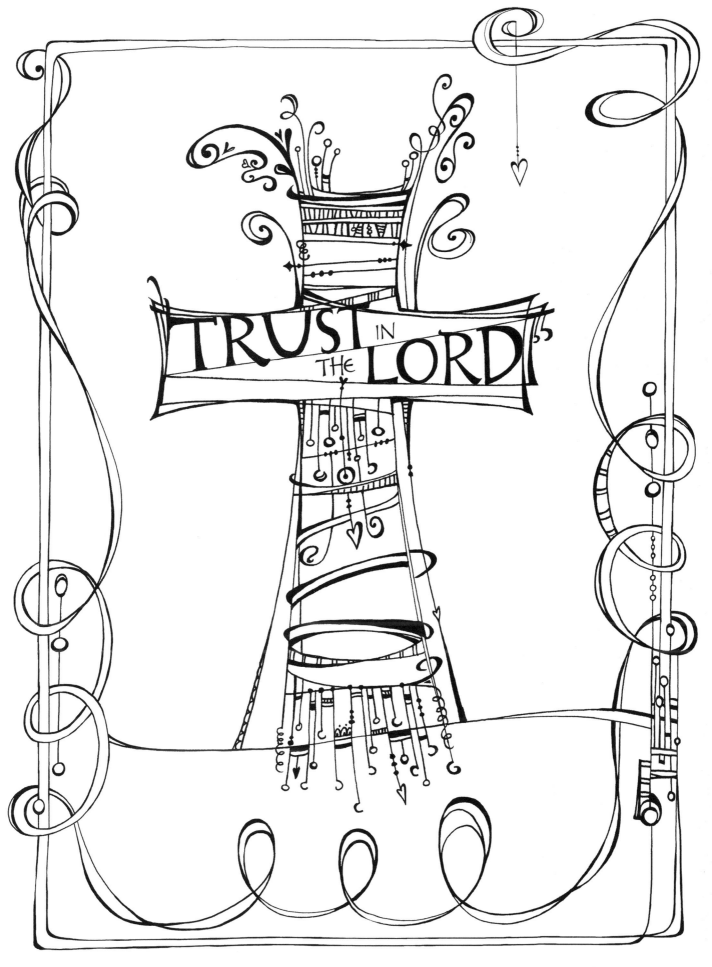

COLOR & CREATIVITY BY

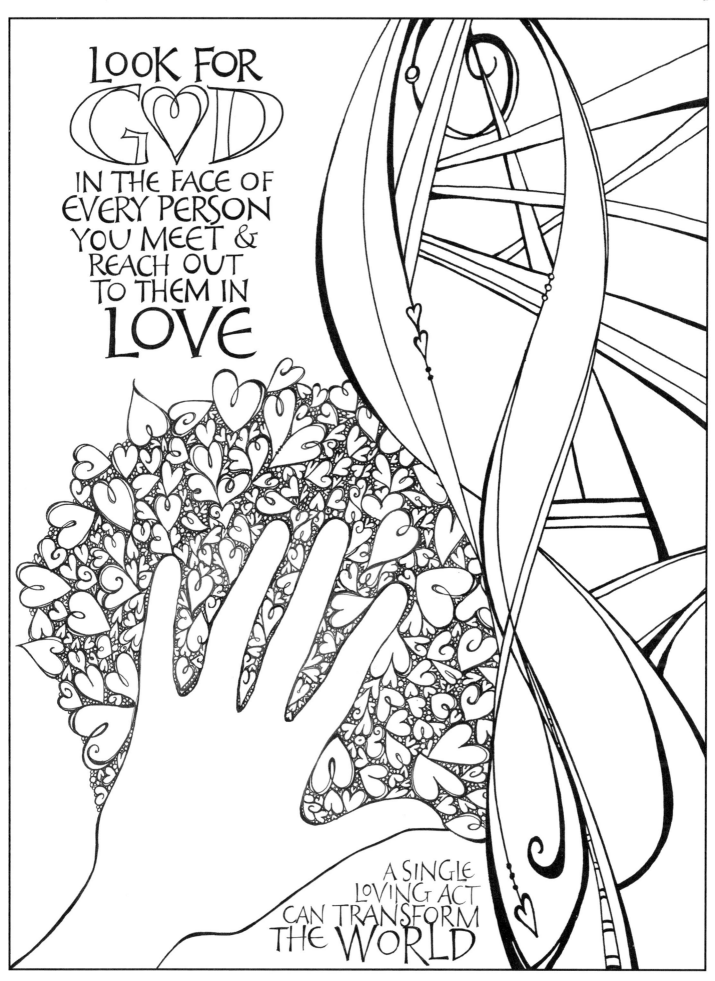

LOOK FOR GOD IN THE FACE OF EVERY PERSON YOU MEET & REACH OUT TO THEM IN LOVE

A SINGLE LOVING ACT CAN TRANSFORM THE WORLD

COLOR & CREATIVITY BY_____

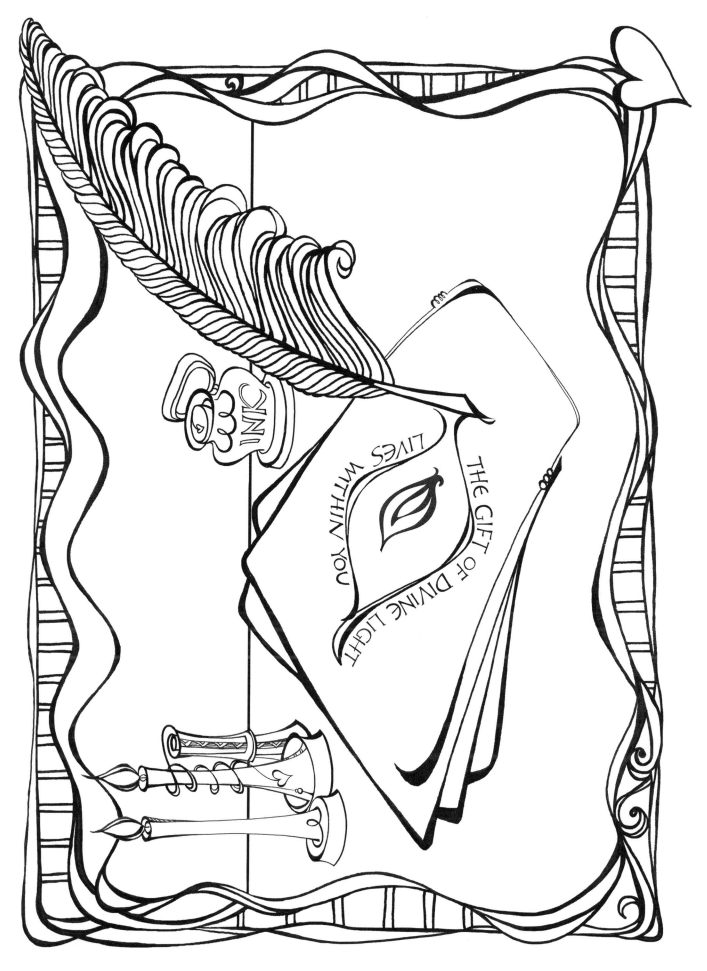

THE GIFT OF DIVINE LIGHT LIVES WITHIN YOU

INK

COLOR & CREATIVITY BY_____

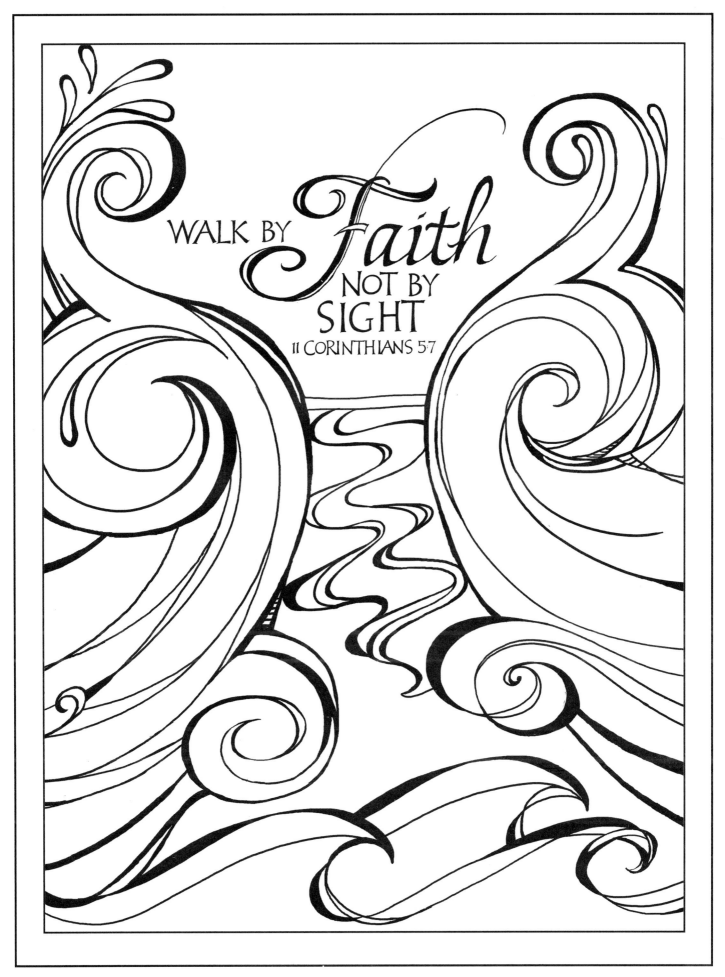

WALK BY *Faith* NOT BY SIGHT
II CORINTHIANS 5:7

COLOR & CREATIVITY BY_____

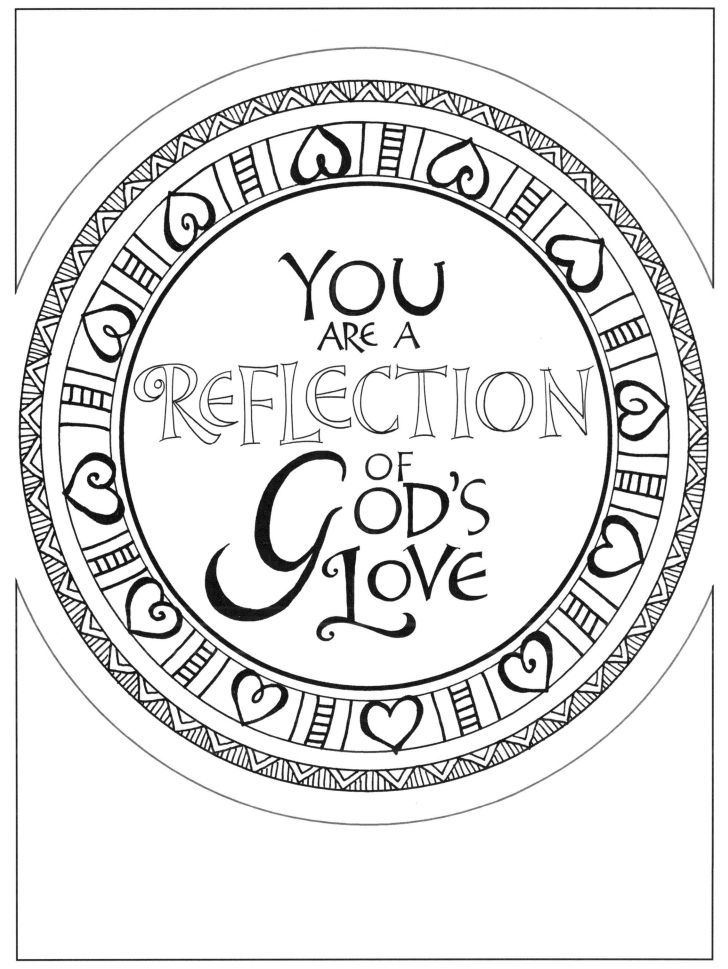

COLOR & CREATIVITY BY_____

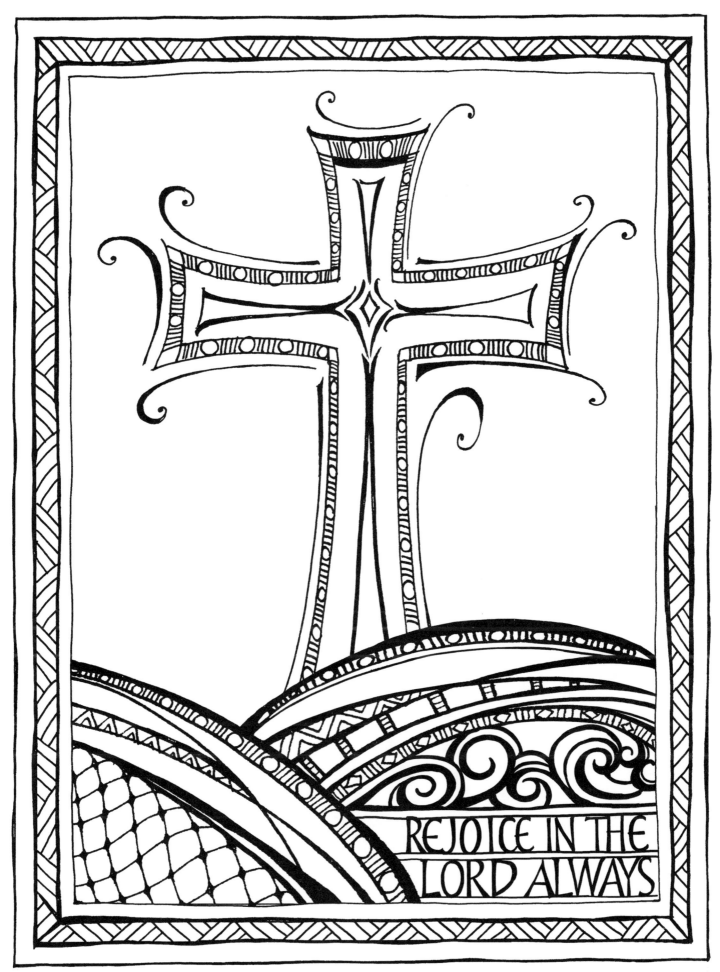

REJOICE IN THE LORD ALWAYS

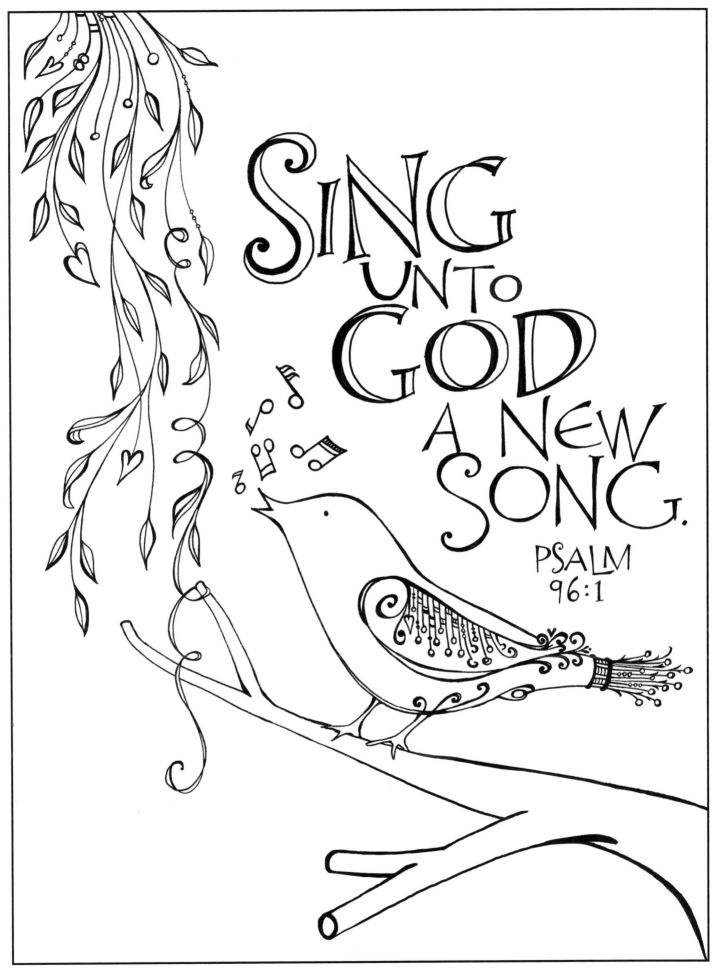

SING UNTO GOD A NEW SONG.

PSALM 96:1

COLOR & CREATIVITY BY_____

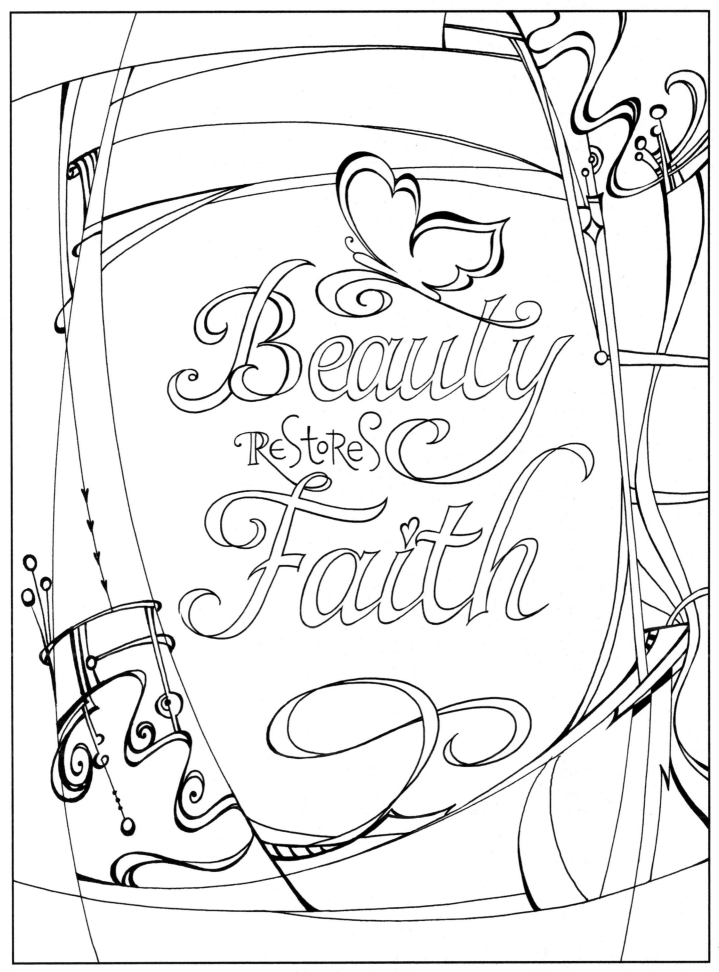

Beauty restores Faith

COLOR & CREATIVITY BY_____

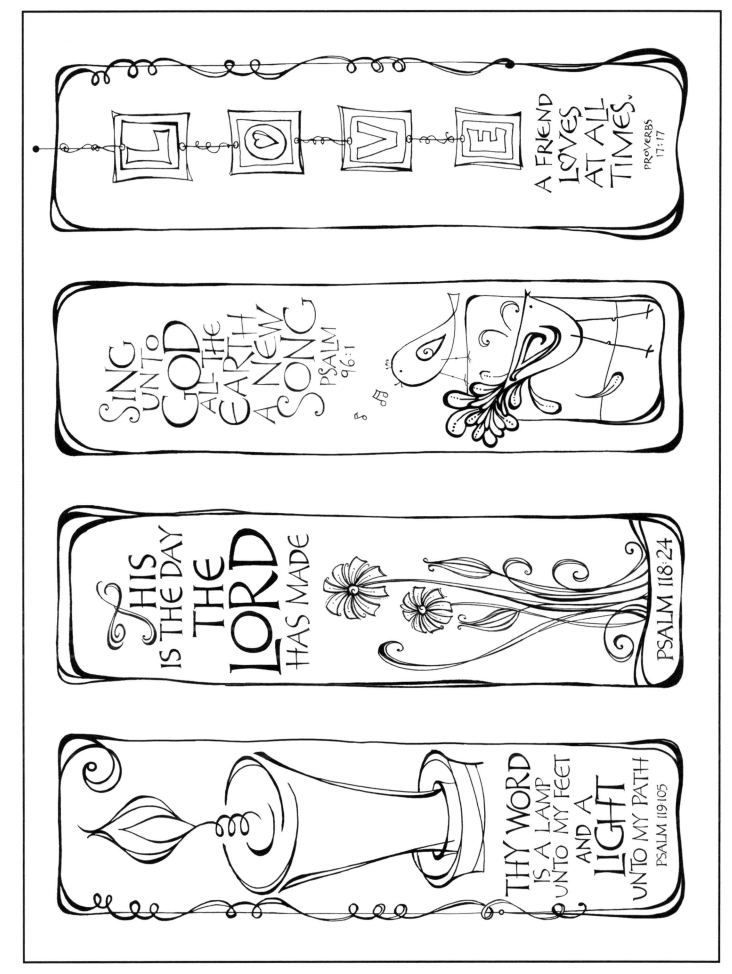

LOVE

A FRIEND LOVES AT ALL TIMES.
PROVERBS 17:17

SING UNTO GOD ALL THE EARTH A NEW SONG PSALM 96:1

THIS IS THE DAY THE LORD HAS MADE
PSALM 118:24

THY WORD IS A LAMP UNTO MY FEET AND A LIGHT UNTO MY PATH
PSALM 119:105

©JOANNE FINK•WWW.ZENSPIRATIONS.COM   COLOR & CREATIVITY BY_____

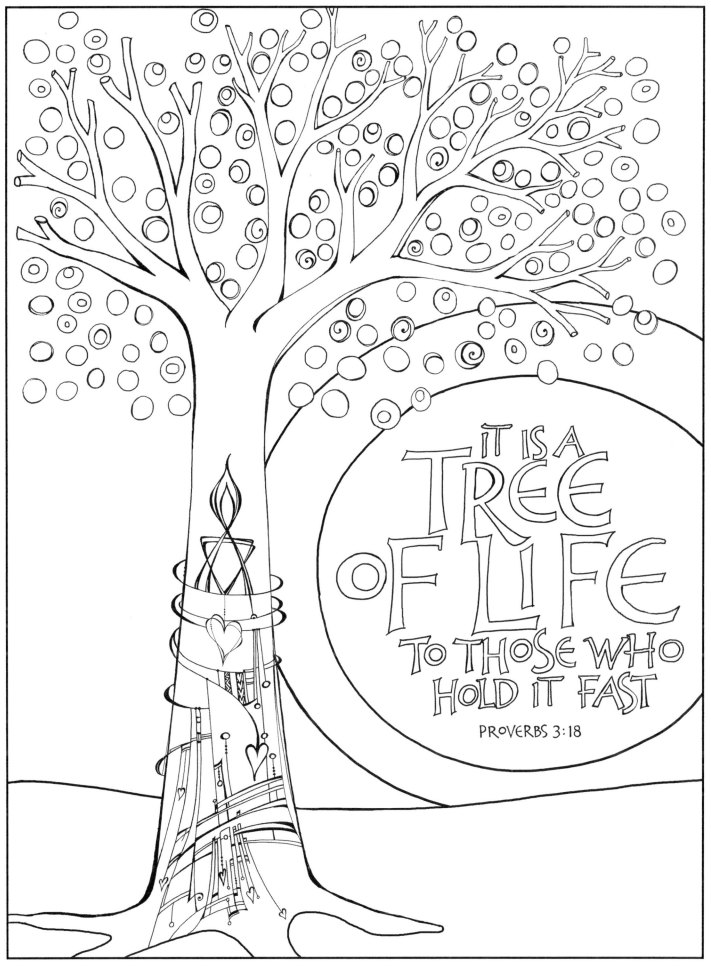

IT IS A TREE OF LIFE TO THOSE WHO HOLD IT FAST

PROVERBS 3:18

COLOR & CREATIVITY BY_____

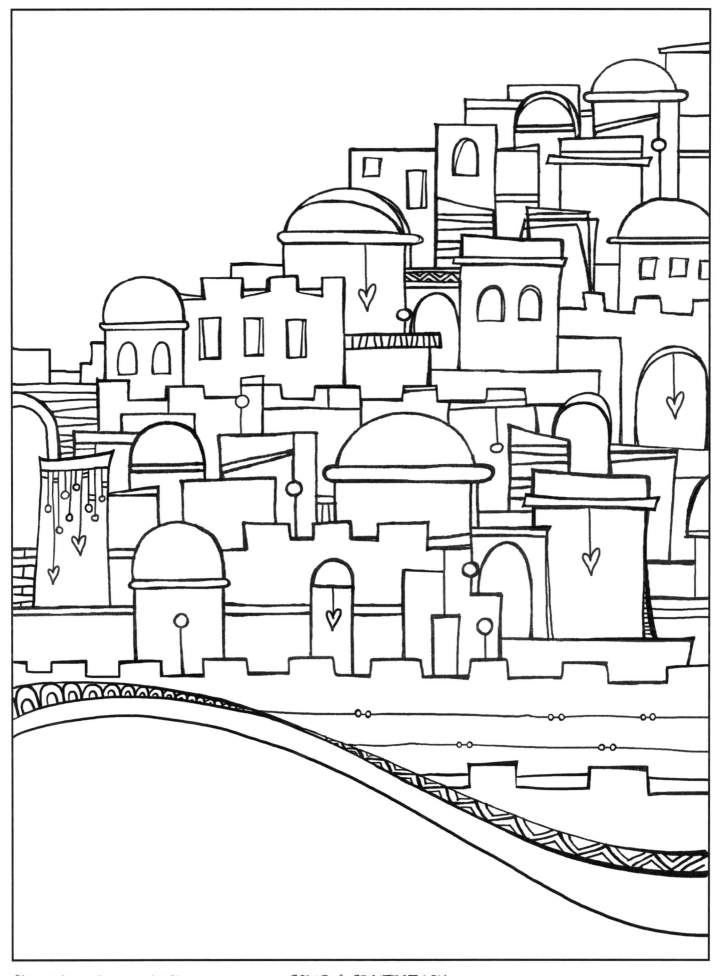

COLOR & CREATIVITY BY_____

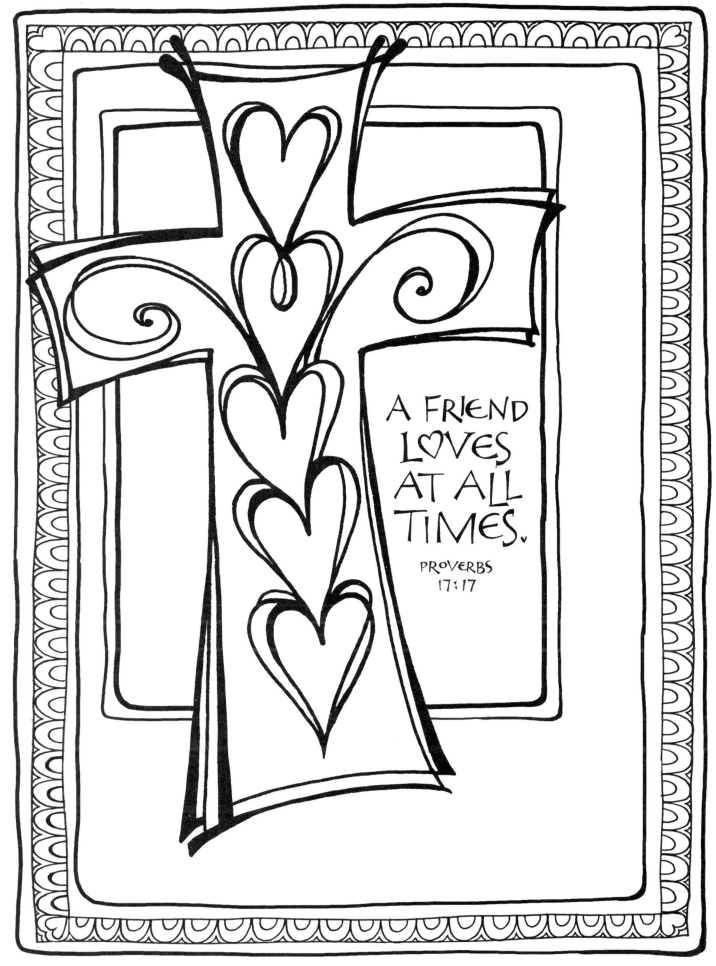

A FRIEND
LOVES
AT ALL
TIMES.

PROVERBS
17:17

COLOR & CREATIVITY BY_____

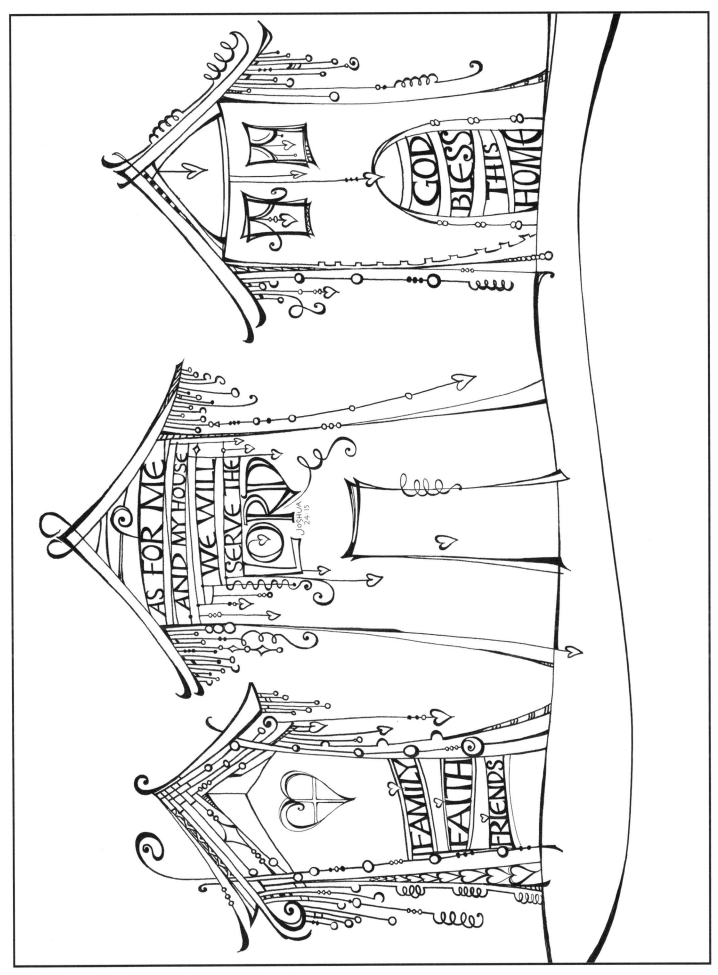

Text visible within the illustration: GOD BLESS THIS HOME · AS FOR ME AND MY HOUSE WE WILL SERVE THE LORD · JOSHUA 24:15 · FAMILY FAITH FRIENDS

COLOR & CREATIVITY BY_____

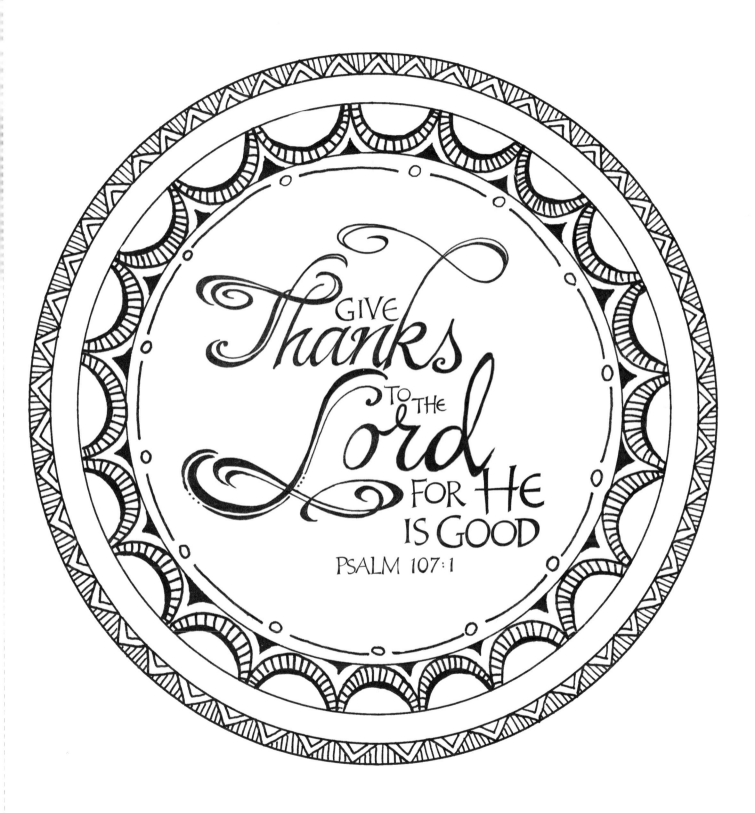

GIVE Thanks TO THE Lord FOR HE IS GOOD

PSALM 107:1

COLOR & CREATIVITY BY_____

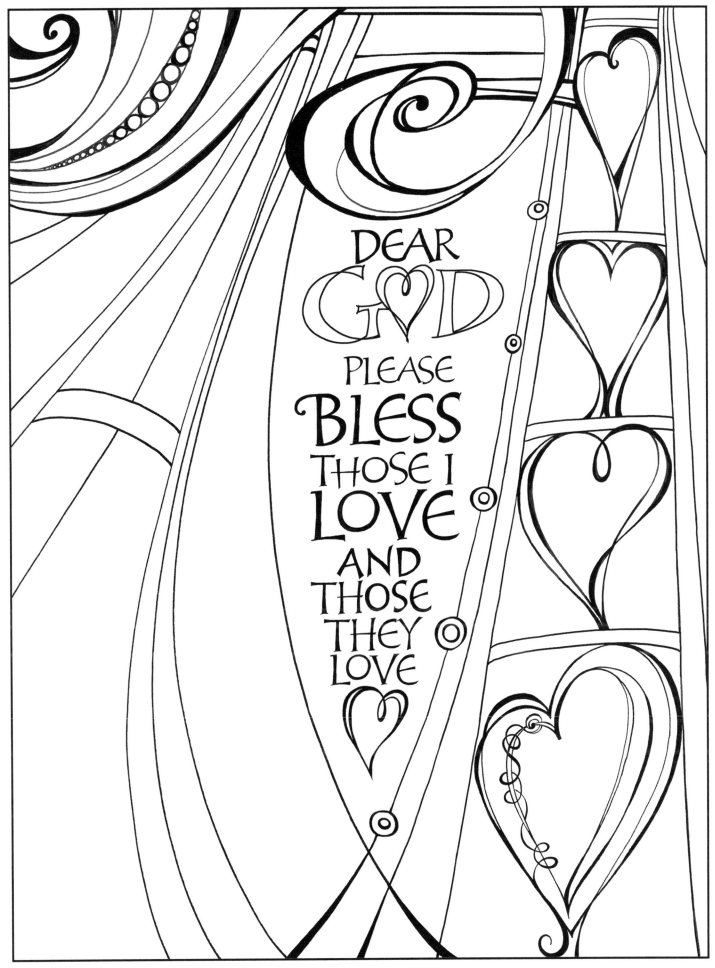

DEAR
GOD
PLEASE
BLESS
THOSE I
LOVE
AND
THOSE
THEY
LOVE

COLOR & CREATIVITY BY_____

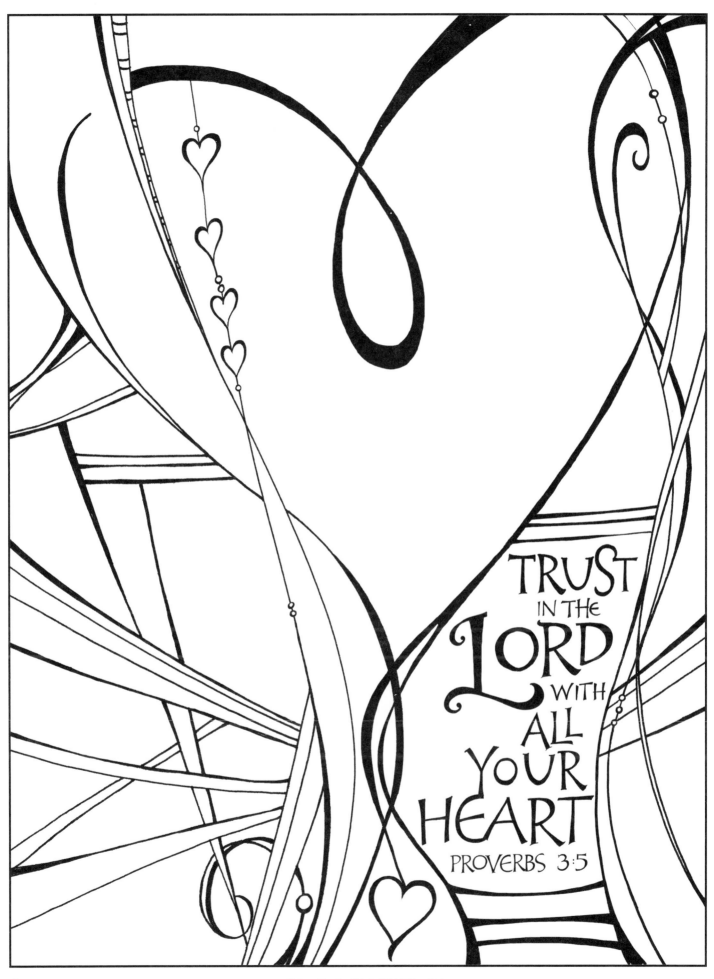

TRUST IN THE LORD WITH ALL YOUR HEART PROVERBS 3:5

COLOR & CREATIVITY BY_____

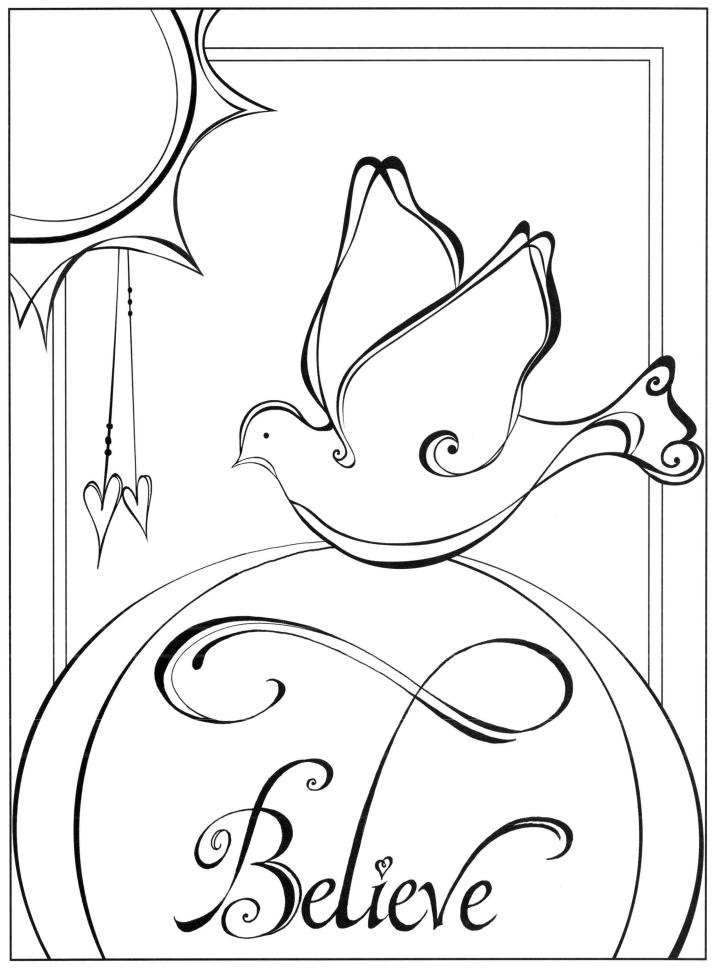

Believe

COLOR & CREATIVITY BY

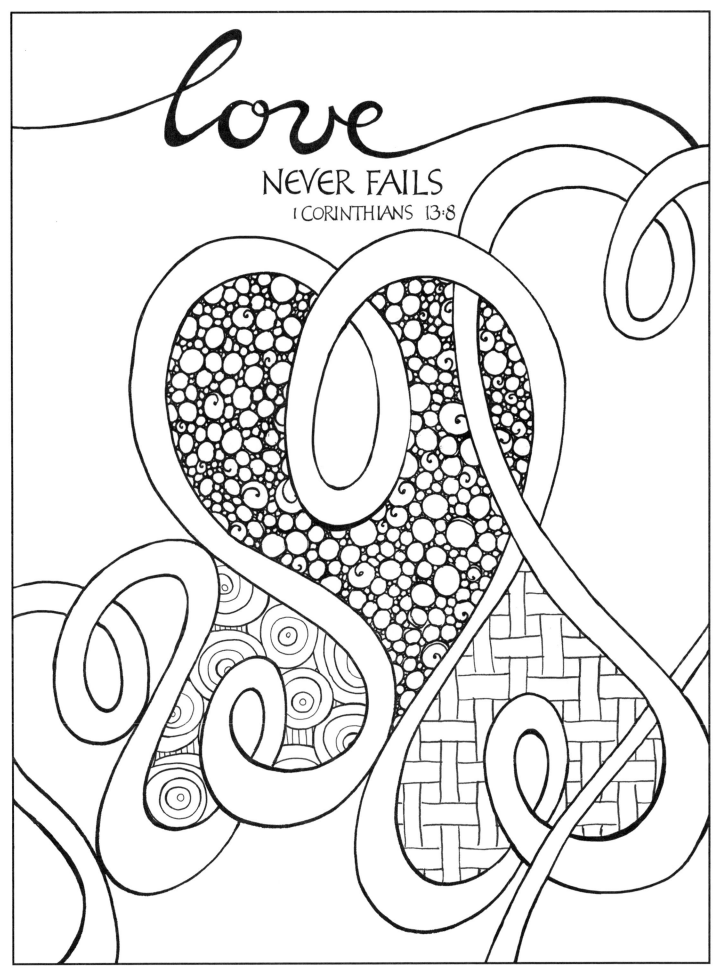

love

NEVER FAILS
1 CORINTHIANS 13:8

COLOR & CREATIVITY BY_____